Live Rich on an Ordinary Income

Dale Chronister

Critical Mass Books
Haymarket, Virginia
www.criticalmasspublishing.com

ISBN: 978-1-947153-31-8

| Cover Design | Eowyn Riggins |
| Interior Layout | Rachel Newhouse |

Contents

Foreword

I met Dale Chronister more than 20 years ago in church. We became friends, colleagues, and co-laborers for the cause of Christ. Since I have known him, Dale has always been passionate about two things—the Word of God and living financially free by applying the principles found in scripture. The information in this book is the same information he shared with me in the late 1990s.

I have read many books about Biblical stewardship and financial freedom over the years, first as a young believer learning the principles of trusting God with my money, and then while pastoring a church and trying to find pertinent material to refer to others. I have also attended some of the best-known financial stewardship classes in the country.

In fact, we hosted both at our church and I can honestly say this material is better than either of them. Dale's material is both applicable to every household and incredibly supportive of the local church. Some programs don't talk about partnering with the local church or any ministry until late in the curriculum, Dale highlights the importance of church support and ministry partnership as a priority in any biblical financial stewardship discussion.

In the years I have known Dale, his passion has been to help people be strong spiritually in such a way that they are fulfilled in their family dynamic, effective in their ministry, and successful in their business so that they can help others do the same. I highly recommend *Live Rich on an Ordinary Income* as an exceptional resource that will empower your life to incredible spiritual and financial health.

KEN SPICER

Pastor with 23 years of vocational ministry
and founder of *Revere Network.*

Introduction

I do not have a business degree, and I have never studied economics at the graduate level. I am not a guru, just an ordinary, hard-working guy. But I do love learning and I have a craving for knowledge. And over the years, I have soaked up material about money and finance like a sponge. I have also put great concepts into practice in my life. This is how I did it—not personal financial advice.

I am also one of those all-too-rare people who knows what it is to be financially free. This hasn't happened in my life because of greed. I'm not a materialistic man. I consider myself a man who has been blessed—by God. I love this verse from the Bible:

> *"The blessing of the Lord makes one rich, and He adds no sorrow with it."*
>
> —PROVERBS 10:22 (NKJV)

I could be a posterchild for that scripture. As a follower of Jesus Christ, I know that none of the knowledge I've picked up about money and finance along the way would be worth a hill of beans to me without my faith. I believe with all my heart that faith is the key factor to ultimate success. What is success anyway? I like this definition: "Success is finding the will of God and then doing it." And the will of God includes His plans for our money and material things.

In the New Testament, the Apostle Paul talks about this:

> *"Now godliness with contentment is great gain. For we brought nothing into this world, and it is certain we can carry nothing out. And having food and clothing, with these we shall be content. But those who desire to be rich fall into temptation and a snare, and into many foolish and harmful lusts which drown men in destruction and perdition. For the love of money is a root of all kinds of evil, for which some have strayed from the faith in their greediness, and pierced themselves through with many sorrows."*
>
> —I TIMOTHY 6:6-10 (NKJV)

Now, you'll notice he made a strong statement about money relating to "all kinds of evil." But make sure you read it closely, he didn't say that the problem was money itself, but rather "the **love** of money." In other words, greed.

How can you tell whether you are operating out of greed? I think the key is also in that passage by Paul. It's one important word: CONTENTMENT. Contentment means, simply, "I have enough." Without this virtue and value in your life, you'll be chasing elusive things and find yourself being quite sad. That's what it means when it says, "pierced themselves through with many sorrows."

Remember, the Proverbs verse I gave you? It said that when God blesses us there is *no* sorrow. I want money, but not with the strings of sadness attached. I want it through the blessings of God. I've written this book to share with you, humbly, some of the things I have learned all the way. And I am dedicating it to the Lord—the source of all the good things in my life.

One thing you need to know, not only am I an unapologetic Christian, I am also someone who believes in, and is very committed to the concept of church. The local church. It is the fertile soil for Kingdom work.

Though the following quote is more than a century old, it still rings true today:

"For money you can have everything it is said. No, that is not true. You can buy food, but not appetite; medicine, but not health; soft beds, but not sleep; knowledge but not intelligence; glitter, but not comfort; fun, but not pleasure; acquaintances, but not friendship; servants, but not faithfulness; grey hair, but not honor; quiet days, but not peace. The shell of

*all things you can get for money. But not the kernel.
That cannot be had for money."*

—ARNE GARBORG

I hope you enjoy and pick up a few things as you read, *Live Rich on an Ordinary Income.*

—DALE CHRONISTER

November 2021

Chapter One

"The Place to Start"

Have you ever visited an out-of-town Mall? Back home, you probably know every nook and cranny of your local shopping center, but when you're someplace else it's unfamiliar territory. So what do you do? You look for a big sign that says "Directory." Let's say, you're looking for the heartbeat of any Mall—the Food Court. And there it is on level B somewhere, according to the map.

So what's the problem?

To get to where you want to be, you first have to know where you are. So you look for a little marker on the directory that says the most important words you need to know before you can reach your destination— *You Are Here.*

Knowing where you are is the first step to getting to where you want to go. And when it comes to your finances, if you're the typical American, you want success, or at least the trappings of success. It's called the American dream. The nice car, the big house, plenty of money set aside for those golden years. You probably want to eat the finest food, and enjoy the best entertainment. You'd love to be able to regularly say things like "spare no expense," and "keep the change."

The specific dreams vary from person to person. One person may have million-dollar dreams, while another person may have some that are more modest. But whatever the case, fulfilling them always begins with knowing where you are, or better—where your money is.

The First Step

It's the first step to creating the greatest financial tool ever invented—a *budget*.

There I said it. That word. It is money to what "diet" is to food. And most of us hate that "D" word because it screams "deprivation" and "deferral," when what we really want is all of it right now. But the "B" word, like its "D" counterpart, is vital to a healthy and happy life. The opposite of such a life is one lived in out-of-control frustration and eventual material and emotional destitution.

A budget is the foundation of financial prosperity.

Do you have a financial budget? By this I mean, do you have it written down somewhere? It's a simple question, but also a gateway to something profound. Maybe you've tried budgeting but it didn't work for you. Or was it that you didn't work *it*? Or maybe you hastily put a budget together, but you left a few things out.

Many people spend too much time thinking about how life would be better if just they could find a better job or somehow make more money. But in reality, there is a case to be made that if you don't take full advantage of wise money management where you are now, things are not likely to get better in the future.

Now, as you begin reading this book, you need to know something about me. I'm a Christ-follower. That's right, I'm an evangelical Christian. So I will bring certain things—you might call them "biases"—to my subject. And I freely admit that I do have a "bias" for the Kingdom of God and I believe God has ordained certain truths or principles that work all the time. One bias I have is the idea of stewardship, how God gives us what we have, our opportunities, our possessions, all of it. And the bottom line is that if we are not good stewards of what He has already given us, He is not likely to be in a hurry to give us more.

Let that sink in for a moment.

A steward is just another word for a *manager*. We are called by God to be good managers of every aspect of our lives—and that includes our money and material possessions.

Tools

There are many great budgeting tools on the Internet, they have basic forms you can use to create yours. Or you can just get a piece of paper out and make great notes. Don't get sidetracked by matters of style. Let's begin.

First, calculate your income—how much do you make. For the spending budget, use your net income. We'll talk about taxes later. So this figure would include your regular pay plus any other streams of income you might have. By the way, one of the things we're going to talk about in this book is how to develop multiple streams of income. But for now, just list any way you currently earn money.

Next, begin a review of all your monthly expenses, things like housing—what it costs to live in your home. These expenses would include your rent or mortgage, the utilities for the house, and any other upkeep costs. Then comes expenses related to your vehicle or vehicles, including fuel and insurance costs. Next comes your grocery bill. Clothing and cosmetic stuff come next. Finally, look at things like entertainment and eating out— including that latte at Starbucks. Count everything. Included under entertainment, list how much you spend on things like cable tv and streaming services. This is a good place to put your cell phone bill if you didn't include it under utilities.

Be sure to include things like life insurance premiums, any student loan payments, and your monthly credit card bills (hopefully you're paying more than the minimum). Don't overlook the small expenditures. Benjamin Franklin said, *"Beware of little expenses; a little leak will sink a great ship."*

Finally, be sure to include one thing that actually should be at the top of the list—giving. I'll talk much more about this a bit later in the book, but learning the principles of generosity is vital to any real financial success.

Be honest about it all—income and outgo. Don't hold back. That would be like lying to your doctor about something related to your pain. He couldn't do a good physical exam without your honesty. The same is true when it comes to a "financial physical."

I guarantee that if you do this "financial physical" right, how much you spent will likely surprise you. You may even be shocked.

Now it's time for the drumroll.

Total up your monthly expenses and your total income. Then subtract your expenses from your income. If you are like many people who have never really worked with a budget, you'll see either a break-even scenario or you'll find yourself upside down.

Of course, if you break even, you'll probably feel good about things, until you realize that you aren't making any real headway. You likely have little or no savings. And you'll be relying on your credit cards the next time a crisis expense comes around the corner. You know that's going to happen at some point.

Having done this exercise you are already setting yourself apart from the norm, sadly. Most people don't know where they are or where they're going.

If You're Self-Employed

People who are self-employed or own their own business understand that sometimes income is sporadic. I know this all-too-well. I have worked for many years as a contractor, so I understand budgets, making payroll, and finding creative ways to make the money stretch and last. There can be times when you don't get paid every week, or sometimes even every month. There have been times when I had to wait three or four months. That's when knowing how to budget comes in handy.

Someone who, for example, owns a landscaping business may be flush with cash during the Spring and Summer but then comes the winter. Budgeting helps this person plan for those lean months. It's the same with people who make the bulk of their income during a short season, like around the holidays, or people who own businesses by the beach during the hot summer.

If you're in this kind of situation the first thing you need to do is to figure out what your monthly needs are—year round. Then, put yourself on a fixed income (budget) and no matter if you have a boatload of money in your account because of seasonal work, you must forget that and pay yourself the same "salary" month after month. You must defer the compensation to spread it out enough to cover the entire year. It takes discipline, but that's what budgeting is—imposing discipline on your money. You control it so the lack of it won't control you.

Mom

My mother raised five kids on the money she made as a waitress. She knew how to budget because she had to. She also taught us how to do it. Remarkably, when she passed on she left all five of us an inheritance. She was an amazing lady. She did menus and lived frugally. She didn't live extravagantly, but we were always comfortable. And she saved every penny she could.

She budgeted our meals every two weeks. A complete meal plan. She shopped on purpose for all the things to make those already-planned meals. Nothing more. She filled the shopping cart with items for the next 14 meals. By the way, one great way to budget money is not to overspend at the grocery store—especially those near-the-checkout impulse purchases. If my mother was alive today, she'd likely love the big-bulk stores, they'd be right up her financial alley.

I was also influenced by my grandfather, who was an executive for the Santa Fe Railroad. We only saw him a few times a year, but he seemed determined to reinforce our mother's example with his own words of wisdom. He would tell us things like, "Kids if you invest $200 every month, at the end of your life you'll be worth a million dollars."

The thing about a budget is that it is self-regulating. You have to figure it out. Everybody is different. You have to go through and cut stuff out. There isn't going to be anyone looking over your shoulder to do it for you. Whether you start taking your lunch or you only do your fingernails once a month, you have to do it.

It is part of being a grownup.

For Better or Worse

Creating a budget can be a particular challenge for married couples. It's a pretty well-known fact that a great many marital arguments have to do with money. Sometimes opposites attract in a marriage, but opposites can also *attack*. It's not uncommon for a couple to include one spender and one saver—or at least someone who is more frugal and less impulsive. Sometimes these differences lead to secrecy, something that is always toxic to any relationship.

Budgeting can be the ultimate test of "for better or worse."

But if you do it right and work through this process it can actually enhance your marriage and lead to the kind of freedom prosperity carries along with it. If you're married, you need to hammer it out. You have to find common ground when it comes to money matters. You have to pick and choose your battles.

The key to every aspect of marriage is complete honesty, and this is particularly true when it comes to money matters. For this to work, there is usually required a "come to Jesus" moment, when all the financial cards are put on the table.

One thing that is helpful for couples is to set up regular times when you track things and go over finances. Even though there may be tension at first, and at times, you will eventually find a way to work together for your marriage's best interest.

Yes, It's Hard—But It's Vital

Why is budgeting so hard when it is such a no-brainer? Why is it hard for people to even get to the point where they think they need it? I think there are a couple of reasons.

First, no one has taught or modeled financial self-regulation—budgeting. In my case, I had my mother and grandfather. How they handled money made a lasting impression on me. They not only talked the talk, but they also walked the walk.

Then, there are those who may understand budgeting in the abstract, but they don't think it is important for them. For others, it's fine. But they prefer to live life without restraints, boundaries, and borders. It's a kind of immaturity.

Or arrested development.

Budgeting tells you where your money is going so you'll never have to wonder where it went.

Here's the bottom line:

If you have no savings,
you're broke.

If you have no retirement assets,
you're broke.

If you spend your whole paycheck on bills,
you're broke.

If you take money out of your savings or retirement regularly,
you're broke.

If you are living paycheck to paycheck,
you're broke.

If you want to be wealthy,
you must CHANGE.

And that change can start only one way—create a budget. You wouldn't go on a trip to somewhere you've never been before without a map. You wouldn't build a house without blueprints. You wouldn't create a great new dish without a recipe. And you can't become prosperous without first creating and following a budget.

You have to do money on purpose. Or, to put it simply: You must tell your money where to go. Rich people know this and follow this principle. Banks know this and follow it. Just try getting a loan without proving you can pay it back. When banks pull your credit report they're looking at expenditures, lines of credit, and late payments. In other words, they want to know how you budget and manage your money.

Chapter Two

"Pay It Upward—and Forward"

No matter how old you are (although, admittedly the younger you start the better), there are two fundamental habits you need to develop and stick to on your way to financial freedom and prosperity. First, you should start giving at least ten percent of your income away (you read that right). Second, you should take the second ten percent and pay it to yourself—savings.

Amos Jacobs grew up in the 1920s in the Detroit area. When he was about ten years old he got a job selling what we from the Midwest call *pop* in a theater. He caught the show business bug. He wanted to be a singer. He had a pretty good voice, and he had a pretty quick wit about him. By the time he was sixteen he was pursuing his dream.

His mother was a devout, churchgoing, God-fearing woman who faithfully took the kids to church. She didn't want her boy to be a showman, she wanted him to start a business, to do something with his life. But his mind was made up, and he would not be deterred.

During one gig he met a girl. They eventually married and started a family, living hand-to-mouth, moving from place to place. Finally, Amos got a break and a good job at a famous club in Detroit. Things were looking up until the day he came home and told his pregnant wife, that he had gotten his notice that day. The club was closing, and he no longer had a job.

He had a child on the way and just $7.85 in his pocket.

The next day was Sunday and he and his wife went to church. Amos prayed, "God, please take care of us." The offering basket was passed and he thought, "I will put something in the basket, I guess." So he pulled a dollar bill from his pocket. Then he felt that God was speaking to him and saying, "I want all seven dollars." So he reached back into his pocket and pulled out the other six dollar bills and put it all in the basket. I am pretty sure his wife looked at him and her face probably said, "Seriously?"

Amos walked out of that church with 85 cents in his pocket and no prospect of a job. He prayed, "Lord, I have done this, but you have to take care of me." The next morning, he got a telephone call. It was an agent who had a radio commercial for him that paid $75. He started shouting for joy. He prayed, "Lord, you keep meeting my needs, I will put you first, and I will do something significant for you, whatever it is you want."

His career started to take off, and he soon decided that Amos Jacobs was not a real celebrity-style name, so he took the first names of two of his brothers as his show business name. He had a brother named Danny and another brother named Thomas.

Danny. Thomas.

Danny Thomas eventually had a dream to build a hospital for children in need, those with life-threatening illnesses considered lost causes, where doctors could do research. In 1958, he broke ground in Memphis, Tennessee, for what is now St. Jude's hospital. They do life-saving and life-changing work.

Do you know where that great institution of healing came from? It came from a man who learned how to give. He did not wait until he was a success to become a giver. *Becoming a giver made him a success.* He did not wait until he was making millions. He did not wait until he was Danny Thomas on *Make Room for Daddy.* He did not wait until he was producing *The Andy Griffith Show, The Dick Van Dyke Show,* and so many others. He did not wait. He acted when he had only $7.85 in his pocket, a pregnant wife, and no job. The little he had, he gave to God. He put God first, by faith, and it revolutionized his life.

Learning to Give

Even more important than budgeting, learning how to give is crucial to ultimate financial prosperity. In fact, it is crucial to life itself. The universe operates on laws, like the law of gravity. And one of the most important laws, according to the Bible is that of sowing and reaping. It's a natural law. And it's a supernatural law. Just as planting a single seed in the soil can yield exponential fruit, so giving is like sowing or planting seed. The Apostle Paul said it this way in his second letter to the Corinthians:

> *"But this I say: He who sows sparingly will also reap sparingly, and he who sows bountifully will also reap bountifully. So let each one give as he purposes in his heart, not grudgingly or of necessity; for God loves a cheerful giver. And God is able to make all grace abound toward you, that you, always having all sufficiency in all things, may have an abundance for every good work."[1]*

As I told you in the previous chapter, my faith certainly informs every area of my life, and that includes how I view and deal with money and material things. So, it should come as no surprise to readers that giving is a gigantic priority in my life. As the Danny Thomas story suggests, it can be a gateway to a healthy kind of prosperity.

I know it is common in books and movies to portray wealthy people as greedy and cynical, but the truth is that most people who have realized their financial dreams have learned how to be generous. According to Forbes Magazine, most of the top givers are also the richest people in America. People such as

---

[1] II Corinthians 9:6-8 (NKJV)

Warren Buffett, Bill and Melinda Gates, and the Walton family (Walmart) contribute billions (yes, billions with a "b") of dollars to charitable causes each year.

And you might be tempted to think that they only started to do this when they became incredibly wealthy, but that's not actually the case. For example, Warren Buffett, who is famously on a quest to give most of his money away, learned the value of giving as a young man growing up in Nebraska.

Although he is pretty much a forgotten figure these days, the story of a man named R. G. LeTourneau is worth noting. He was a businessman who developed a line of earth-moving equipment. In fact, he had almost 300 inventions and patents. He started to give at the beginning of his career and increased the percentage over the years. Eventually, he was giving 90% of his income to the work of the Kingdom of God. He said it this way, using imagery from his work creating machines to move dirt around: *"I shovel out the money, and God shovels it back—but God has a bigger shovel."*

It's important to say that the size of your sacrifice is much more important than the size of the gift. True giving is always *proportional.* Jesus emphasized this concept:

> *"Jesus sat down opposite the place where the offerings were put and watched the crowd putting their money into the temple treasury. Many rich people threw in large amounts. But a poor widow came and put in two very small copper coins, worth only a few cents.*

Calling his disciples to him, Jesus said, 'Truly I tell you, this poor widow has put more into the treasury than all the others. They all gave out of their wealth; but she, out of her poverty, put in everything—all she had to live on.'"

—MARK 12:41-45 (NIV)

Of course, this debunks the idea that you should wait until you have a lot of money to start giving. In fact, the sooner you learn and cultivate this habit, the better. As I said, true giving is always proportional.

Tithing

When we talk about giving ten percent of your income away, we're talking about something that goes back more than 3,000 years—tithing. The word tithe means *the tenth part.* So when we talk about this, we mean giving ten percent of our regular income back to God. To my mind, this means supporting my local church—that's one of my faith values. But, as we saw with the Danny Thomas story, the principle (giving away ten percent) works wherever it's tried. You don't have to give like I do. But you do have to give to be financially free and prosperous.

The first time we see someone give a tithe is way back in the book of Genesis—long before the Ten Commandments came down from the mountain. Abraham had returned from a

18

successful raid to rescue his nephew Lot who had been kidnapped. Not only did he get his nephew back, but he completely defeated the army that took him. He also acquired some "spoils of war." Then, he meets a man of God named Melchizedek, to whom he gave ten percent of what he had acquired—a tithe. It is the way to put first things first in your finances.

When we practice tithing, something powerful happens. It's like we have unlocked something mysterious, an almost miraculous power. In fact, there is a passage of scripture that tells us God opens the "windows of heaven" as His response to tithing.[2]

Quite frankly, it's a sweet deal.

It is also the epitome of wisdom. Consider what the "wisdom" book of the Bible says:

> *"One gives freely, yet grows all the richer; another withholds what he should give, and only suffers want."*

> —PROVERBS 11:24

[2] Malachi 3:10

19

Pay Yourself

The second part of the equation—the way to move your life toward financial freedom and prosperity—is to take the second tenth of your income and give it back to yourself in the form of savings and investments.

This is another principle that will help you wherever you are on your journey in life, but as with tithing, it's particularly powerful when you start young. If you are now in your 40s or 50s, can you imagine what your financial bottom line would look like if you had started to do this in your 20s, or even your teens when you were starting your career.

There are several ways to start saving ten percent of your income. First, you have to prioritize your financial goals for the long term. This is crucial. I know there is a lot of value under certain circumstances for looking at life "one day at a time," but there is also a case to be made for having the kind of long-term goals that pull you toward them. They must, therefore, be compelling.

Next, you need to look for ways to cut your spending. You'll be amazed at how making modest lifestyle changes can make a significant difference. Maybe you need to cancel a few subscriptions, or cut out that daily *Starbucks* premium beverage, or decide to eat out less—you might even brown-bag your lunch and take it to work. Much of this will, of course, become clear through the budgeting exercises you will have already done. Once you examine every regular expenditure in detail, you'll easily see what is "fat" and what is "lean." Cutting out the fat and living on the lean will put you well on the path to that ten percent invest-in-yourself goal.

I think one of the keys to success with this is not to think of it as deprivation or sacrifice, but as more of an investment in yourself. I'll talk more about this in a later chapter about your "safety net."

Here's a hard truth. When we look at the Bible hermeneutically (interpretively) and apply it to our lives, it's clear that our choices make all the difference. We get to choose if we want to work with God and follow His plan for our lives. We get to choose if we want God's help with our finances. For me, I want His help. Even more, I need it. I want to be led to the best deals, I want a check in my spirit when something isn't right. On that great and glorious day when we stand and give account, I'm not going to be the one who says I didn't believe Him enough to invest in His Kingdom. The greatest deception in life is self-deception. If God doesn't have access to your money, He probably doesn't have access to your heart. It's a Power Principle—we are not what we say, we are what we do. God is gracious, and He will let us do it on our own.

We get to choose how wealthy we become. It's no one else fault. It's not how much money we make, it's about what we do with that money. If we refuse to pay ourselves and reinvest there is only one person to blame for.

Some Money Stats

- $50 a month for 40 years is 1.550 million = $ 1.65 a day
- $100 a month for 40 years is 3.1 million = $ 3.20 a day
- $203 a month for 30 years is 1.1 million = $ 6.70 a day
- $203 a month for 40 years is 4.5 million
- $780 a month for 20 years is 960 thousand = $ 25.70 a day
- 30 years is 4 million
- 40 years is 16,677 million

All of these numbers are based on earning 15%. The first question is where to get 15%. This is why you have to pick up a book or at least study what other people are doing. But be forewarned, markets change and we have to change with them. This is why we have to be engaged and not just sitting on the sidelines.

We all start and end in different places, so just like a trip across the country, you look at the map to know where you are. If there is road construction, or a road is closed, or bad weather, you take an alternate route. It's the same with your money. If you stay engaged you will do better in the long run.

We must develop and master discipline and maturity. So, yes a little money over a long period can become a boatload of cash.

Finally, one practical step you can take is to make your saving automatic. In other words, set things up with your bank where you have that ten percent "invest" deducted each time you are paid and routing it into some kind of savings account. The kind of account depends on a lot of factors, but we'll hit those a bit later in the book.

For now, remember these simple thoughts: Give God the first tenth, save the second tenth, and live on the 80% that remains.

You might find that difficult to wrap your mind around, at first. But you need to realize that if you put giving first in your finances, you have released a particular power, one that results in the supernatural stretching of the remaining finances.

Let me put it this way. When you put giving first, you will notice that the amount you have left will go further than the original 100% would have had you spent it all on yourself.

> "Give, and it will be given to you: good measure, pressed down, shaken together, and running over will be put into your bosom. For with the same measure that you use, it will be measured back to you."
>
> —LUKE 6:38 (NKJV)

> "The blessing of the Lord makes rich, and he adds no sorrow with it."
>
> — PROVERBS 10:22 (ESV)

Chapter Three

"Make the Best with What You Have"

One of my favorites stories in the Bible is the one about a shepherd boy named David and how he defeated a giant named Goliath. It is the classic underdog wins story, one that still resonates today as a metaphor fitting any situation where someone seems to be coming up against insurmountable challenges or overwhelming odds.

Goliath, the champion of the Philistines, had been harassing Israel's army for quite some time. The Israelites were getting ready for a battle against the Philistines, the valley of Elah separating the two armies, each of which stood on a mountain. Goliath was a giant of over nine feet in height, and he wore heavy armor and carried a huge spear. Every morning, he walked out and challenged the Israelite army to send one soldier to fight a representative battle. If Goliath beat the

Israelite, the Philistines would win, but if the Israelite champion was victorious, the Israelites would win.

Of course, to a man, the Israelites feared the mighty warrior. Even their king, Saul, was intimidated. But the young shepherd-boy David accepted the challenge, stepping out to face Goliath armed only with his staff, a sling, and five smooth stones he took from the nearby brook, placing them in his shepherd's bag.

Goliath cursed David, calling up his gods against the boy, but David replied that *his* God, the Lord, would support him. These words made Goliath angry, so he rushed towards the young boy. I like how bestselling author, Malcolm Gladwell describes it in his book, *David and Goliath: Underdogs, Misfits, and the Art of Battling Giants*:

> *"He runs toward Goliath, because without armor he has speed and maneuverability. He puts a rock into his sling and whips it around and around, faster and faster at six or seven revolutions per second, aiming his projectile at Goliath's forehead—the giant's only point of vulnerability. Eitan Hirsch, a ballistics expert with the Israeli Defense Forces, recently did a series of calculations showing that a typical-size stone hurled by an expert slinger at a distance of thirty-five meters would have hit Goliath's head with a velocity of thirty-four meters per second—more than enough to penetrate his skull and render him unconscious or*

dead. In terms of stopping power, that is equivalent to a fair-sized handgun."[3]

So David, in effect, had brought a pistol to a sword fight.

Five smooth stones—they're what David had selected from a nearby brook for the task. Why five? Well, maybe it was just in case Goliath survived the first blow, or it missed the target. But most likely it was because of something we learn later in the Bible, that Goliath had four brothers just as big as he was.

Whatever the case—and the point of this story for this book—the stones were tools to David. He didn't approach the giant wearing someone else's armor or using things he did not understand. He knew his craft and leveraged it to ultimate success.

David found his craft and did his best—with just Five Smooth Stones.

Your Five Smooth Stones

You can be like David, slaying the giants of poverty and mediocrity. To get ahead of the curve financially, you have to find ways to create income, more income than that from a nine to five job. You need a side gig, or maybe even two or three. And

---

[3] *David and Goliath: Underdogs, Misfits, and the Art of Battling Giants*, Malcolm Gladwell, p. 276

this starts by using *Five Smooth Stones*—meaning your own unique skills and gifts.

Do you know what you're good at? Some people do, and they're the ones who get ahead. They don't waste a lot of time on something they can't do well—unless learning about it or acquiring a new skill will help them achieve their larger purpose.

So, just how do you figure all this out? Well, you might start by asking yourself some questions. What do I do that requires so little effort that it sort of comes naturally? When you are able to answer this simple question you are on your way to figuring out how to monetize it.

What do other people associate me with? Sometimes other people can be more objective about us than we are about ourselves. They'll see things we can miss. And sometimes they just are there to reinforce the obvious. Do people ask you to help them out in specific areas? That may involve a skill you can ultimately monetize.

When someone has seen a gift in me, how have I used it? Maybe you're a good storyteller and people love that about you. But have you ever tried to write the stories down? Maybe you could write a novel.

The bottom line is that we are born with everything we need already inside us—skills, talents, and abilities that will support us throughout our lives. This is why we're naturally drawn to certain things and not others. It's why we possess certain abilities and perspectives. It's what makes us laugh at some things and cry at others. At times we may forget, but when we remember, it initiates *synchronicity* in our lives. Coined by the famous psychologist Carl Jung, synchronicity means, "A meaningful coincidence of two or more events where something other than the probability of chance is involved."

Life is not a random series of events. We are all here by design in a web of complexity created to help us learn and grow with each experience. When looking deep within we can more clearly consider our place in this world. Recognizing that no life is wasted, there are lessons to be learned in every kind of life. Every life has meaning simply by living it.

One way to recognize your gifts is to look back at when you were a child. What did you enjoy without being told to do it? What were you naturally good at in school? Learn to recognize what has been unique in you and bring it with you wherever you go. Do people ever turn to you for guidance, comfort, or even for a laugh because of your unique perspective on things? Do you have an upbeat attitude or a sense of adventure? Are you a good listener or naturally organized? Do your talents lie in gardening or are animals naturally drawn to you? Are you good at building things or better at demolition?

Keep asking yourself good questions.

What skills and abilities do you admire in others? What do others tell you they admire in you? Identify the special gifts you bring to your relationships and interactions with others.

In what ways can you improve on your strengths? What abilities have you cultivated in yourself that you first admired in others? What makes you happy? Find ways to boost the natural gifts with which you were born.

Recharge Your Life

We've all known kids and then adults who seemed to be unable to grasp or retain information in one field, yet become an expert in another field. What makes the difference? Their level of interest. What captures your interest and captivates your mind?

Networking is another way to discover and grow your skills. This is one of the most important skills you can develop. It can also be an enjoyable experience, bringing value to your work. Networking consists of interacting with professional contacts to share information and help each other. It doesn't always have to be in a formal setting. There are many ways to network, from handing out your business cards to chatting with someone at an industry event.

Such events tend to be filled with professionals and they allow you the opportunity to find new business opportunities. Small and medium-sized businesses find this particularly helpful.

Business relationships are based on trust. This leads to credibility. If you can form trustworthy relationships, you're more likely to deal with them in the future. This can be great for your career. When building your career, it's important to be visible to others - from work colleagues to potential employers.

By attending networking events, you'll build your status within the community by building professional relationships and sharing your knowledge on topics you're familiar with, as well as providing your unique perspective on different areas of business.

Then, never forget the value of blooming where you are planted. Sometimes the best life strategy is to find a way to fall in love with what you are now doing and forget trying to chase greener grass somewhere else. We can't always choose the cards that have been dealt to us, but we can learn to play them better. It's like that old saying, "Life ain't in holding a good hand, but in playing a poor hand well."

Acres of Diamonds

If you've never read the classic book, *Acres of Diamonds*, by Russell Conwell, you need to get a copy and devour it. Conwell, a Baptist minister who went on to become the founder of Temple University in Philadelphia, shared a powerful story with an even more powerful lesson:

> *There was once a wealthy man named Ali Hafed who lived not far from the River Indus. "He was contented because he was wealthy, and wealthy because he was contented." One day a priest visited Ali Hafed and told him about diamonds. Ali Hafed heard all about diamonds, how much they were worth, and went to*

his bed that night as a poor man. He had not lost anything, but he was poor because he was discontented, and discontented because he feared he was poor. Ali Hafed sold his farm, left his family, and traveled to Palestine and then to Europe searching for diamonds. He did not find them. His health and his wealth failed him. Dejected, he cast himself into the sea to death.

One day, the man who had purchased Ali Hafed's farm found a curious sparkling stone in a stream that cut through his land. It was a diamond. Digging produced more diamonds — acres of diamonds, in fact. This, according to the parable, was the discovery of the famed diamonds of Golconda.

Are you one of those people who look for diamonds in faraway places? Is the grass really greener there? Is there an opportunity that has been in front of you all the time? Have you taken stock of your life lately? Perhaps there are diamonds sitting just outside your back door. Now I'm not suggesting you physically go and start digging up your backyard, as the story says, so how can you find the acres of diamonds in your own backyard?

Each of us is right in the middle of our own Acres of Diamonds, if only we would realize it and develop the ground we are standing on before charging off in search of greener pastures.

Opportunity does not just come along – it is there all the time – we just have to see it. In life, when we go searching for "something," we should know what that "something" looks, smells and tastes like so that we can recognize it when we find it. Before we give up what we already have, make sure that what we're getting is better than what we already have.

Although can't always choose the cards we've been dealt, but we can learn to play them better. Like a flower that grows through a crack in the sidewalk, sometimes we have to make the best of our current, and maybe even long-term, situation.

You may not be where you want to be in life right now. You have a job that doesn't spark your passion, but don't let that stop you from improving yourself and how you carry it out day-to -day.

Then dream some after you get off work. Keeping our dreams alive lifts the human spirit. But how can we deal with the fact that sometimes we may have to tolerate something that we do not like before eventually getting where we want to go?

Maybe you can quit your job to follow a dream. Dreams take time. But instead of getting bitter and upset about your circumstances, why not try blooming where you have been planted? You see, I firmly believe that every season of life prepares us for the next one. Where you are now provides you with vital life lessons you'll find yourself using in your next adventure.

When Michael Crichton, the writer of *Jurassic Park*, and numerous other bestsellers, was asked how his medical training helped him as a writer, he said, "Being a doctor is good preparation for this because it teaches you to deal with the kind of life you will inevitably have. It teaches you to work well when you haven't had enough sleep. It teaches you to work well when you are on your feet. It teaches you to make decisions and live by them."

You see, each chapter in your life builds a foundation for the next chapter. So you can either feel sorry for yourself and wonder why you're not where you want to be or you can look at your current situation as a classroom. What is this here to teach me? How can I use this experience to help me toward my ultimate goal?

If you are in a difficult place right now, you can find ways to shine your light to drown out the darkness. Keep working toward what is coming next. And try to understand that your ultimate destiny is not at all determined by present circumstances.

By the way, blooming where you are planted means you have to commit to a life of zero complaints. No one likes to be around a complainer, anywhere. No complainer is truly content. Your job and circumstances may not be ideal right now. But you have to decide for yourself what you can change and what you cannot. I like what Maya Angelou said, "If you don't like something, change it. If you can't change it, change your attitude about it."

Indeed.

Maybe the people who work around you are not doing their best. Instead of expecting others to change, learn to change yourself. Don't let small get under your skin. Like the eye at the center of a hurricane, keep your calm even when the world around you is swirling.

As Steve Jobs once said, "You cannot connect the dots looking forward; you can only connect them looking backward. So you have to trust that the dots will somehow connect in the future."

Learn to bloom where you are planted. If you find yourself planted under a sidewalk, look for a crack in the concrete and find your way out. But no matter what—choose to bloom.

Chapter Four

"Digging Out of Debt"

In order to build wealth you must get your debt under control. This is vital to your budget and to help you with saving your money. Paying down your debt is another way of investing in yourself. Among the negative and unhealthy effects of debt is how it puts pressure on us—financially and emotionally. It is a burden that can become an albatross around our necks.

Even paying off the smallest credit card can provide a sense of relief and reinforce the idea that there is light at the end of your financial tunnel. When you decide to make your coffee at home and save that Starbucks money for debt retirement it can be quite liberating.

Our easy credit and easy debt culture have made it easy for the average American to live, as the old saying goes, "Big hat, no cattle." In other words, all talk and image with little reality to back it all up. It's like that song written by Randy Newman:

Since I was a child
I've tried to be what I am not
I've lied and I've enjoyed it all my life
I lied to my dear mother
To my sisters and my brother
And now I'm lying to my children and my wife
Big Hat, no cattle...

If you're going for status, then at least make sure your image is backed up by reality. And one of the most important things to do to start building the right image is to dig yourself out of debt.

You need to understand how debt compounds. Debt left untreated inevitably leads to more debt. Financial experts refer to this as "debt-spiral." It's defined as situation where someone sees debt increase in an out-of-control way. When someone reaches this point, they will actually take on more debt. They rationalize it by assuming that everybody has high balances on their credit cards. In fact, much of the world thinks debt is a normal and healthy thing. It's not. Unresolved debt eventually becomes unsustainable and many times leads to default and even bankruptcy.

Ben Franklin said: "Rather go to bed supperless than rise in debt."

Your journey to becoming debt-free begins with gathering all your credit bills and calculating and itemizing everything you owe to anyone. Write it all down—the balance owed, the minimum payment, the interest rate and charges, and how long you've had the obligation.

Then, ask yourself a hard question and answer it honestly—is there something secured by debt that you can sell to eliminate some monthly debt? For some people, this may mean letting go of a second car—and car payment. It's possible to free up several hundred dollars per month in this way, and then apply those funds to your unsecured debt—read: credit cards.

What would we do without them? We do actually need them. It's hard to do things like renting a car without them. But swiping and tapping those little plastic cards can lead to big problems. You can buy everything you need with a card—and more. Much more. And it is the "more" that gets you in trouble.

Whatever you don't pay back each month becomes credit card debt. While carrying a balance on your credit card isn't bad in every instance, you need a game plan to make sure you don't become a slave to interest. Credit cards can be wonderful servants, but they make horrible masters.

If you use cards for convenience, but then pay them off each month, then they're not a problem. But when you use them to live beyond your means ("Big hat, No cattle"), with no real plan to pay them off, you are putting yourself in financial peril. It is so easy to use credit cards irresponsibly and things can quickly spiral out of control. Because what you're spending doesn't immediately come out of your bank account, it doesn't hurt.

But it will come back to bite you.

Credit cards are notorious for their high interest rates. Usually much higher than what you pay on an automobile loan or a home mortgage. It's not unusual for a credit card to carry a rate of close to twenty percent. And if you only pay the suggested "minimum payment" from the credit card company, you can theoretically be in debt to them for a decade or more. And ignoring the problem by burying your head in the sand will only make matters worse.

You need to remember that none of your long-term financial goals or dreams can be achieved until you dig yourself out of debt.

Here are gems from Warren Buffett:

"We make decisions every day, our daily decisions compound and create our future."

"If you don't have discipline, you're not in control of your decisions."

"You're controlled by your moods and emotions, which lead to poor decision making."

So Where Do You Start? Stop Spending

Many financial planners suggest focusing on the card that carries the highest interest rate, which can be a healthy choice. But I suggest that you begin with the card that has the *smallest balance*. Why? Because this will create an early "win" in your journey to becoming debt-free. And don't underestimate how important it is to see yourself making progress. Small victories are victories, nonetheless.

While you are paying big chunks on that small card, just pay the minimum on the others. I know that may sound like you're not making progress, but you are. Once that small card is paid off, then take the money you were paying on that card and start applying it to the next smallest. And, so on, and so on. It's like putting your credit cards in a pyramid. You pay the top parts off first, then the middle parts, then—when you have all that monthly money to work with by not having all those small cards to pay—you tackle the big ones at the bottom with larger monthly payments.

By the way, it may seem like a good idea to close your card after you've paid it off, but this is not a great idea. Your credit score is calculated based on the amount of credit you are using versus the total amount of credit in your name. Once you close the card, there is less credit in your name. This will cause your debt utilization ratio to increase, which can hurt you in the end. It's also important to maintain a long length of credit history, so keeping your card open will improve your score, too. Just cut the card up, but keep the account open.

Don't Be Like the Government

Of course, debt is a way of life in America. I mean, just look at how our government does its business—debt upon debt upon debt. It's like "spend now, pay later" is in our national DNA. Nearly eight out of every ten of our fellow citizens have debts and the average amount is nearly $70,000 per person.

But debt is a trap. It ties up your money so you can't do all the things you really want to do. And when I talk about debt, I am speaking mostly about unsecured debt—things like credit cards, not necessarily secured debts like mortgages or car loans. But they can be problematic, as well. One thing I advocate is when you get your credit cards paid off, then take that money to work on paying off your house!

Carrying a boatload of debt ties up your income. Paying it down and ultimately off will have many benefits. First, you'll have more disposable income every month. This will have a positive impact on your lifestyle. And when it comes time to remodel your home or anything else that strikes your fancy, you'll have the money to pay cash for it.

Being debt-free will also help you to become more productive—at work and at home. It's a fact that being overwhelmed by debt can hinder you on the job. You worry at night and lose sleep, which hinders your productivity. And when things really get bad, you can even have debt collectors calling your work, or even have your wages garnished. Bosses don't like that. And trying to get a new job may involve a check of your credit. Many employers won't take a chance on someone who doesn't manage money well.

Debt can be stressful, and stress can lead to a whole array of emotional and physical problems. The daily pressure to pay things off can become paralyzing. Getting free from debt can be a huge relief. Can being debt-free lower your blood pressure? I sure can't hurt it.

By the way, debt is never good in a marriage. Issues will money always lead to strife and strain. In fact, arguing about financial matters places the biggest strain on a marriage. It drains your energy. But working together to get out of debt can strengthen the marital bond.

Paying things off may make it easier for you to consider retirement much earlier than you thought possible. Frankly, having more money available to set aside for your future needs can only serve to accelerate plans for your "golden years." This is the ultimate investment in yourself,

And, having your debts paid off puts you in a much better position to "be there" for others in your life when they have needs. You'll also be able to help them deal with their own financial challenges by teaching and modeling what you have learned and done.

Pick Up the Shovel

Let me finish this chapter with some practical ways you can find the money to begin digging out of debt.

First, take a good long look at things like entertainment (your cable bill, streaming services, etc.). There is a lot of redundancy out there where you can find the same shows available from different streaming services. You don't need all the services. Pick one. Lose the rest.

How about eating out? It has always been more expensive than home-cooked meals, but since the recent pandemic, it has gotten worse. Menu prices are soaring (of course, due to their own increased costs). Choosing to cut your "eating out" occasions in half, or even less, can free up significant funds. Meal planning can also help save money at the grocery store. You might even consider brown-bagging it at work instead of eating out or ordering in.

Do you like books? Possibly, you like shopping for them on Amazon, where it is easy to purchase a title with the click of a mouse. But when was the last time you had a library card? I know one guy who saved nearly $1,000 per year by getting his reading material from the local public library than at the bookstore or via the internet.

Junk food is inherently more expensive than the good stuff. This is another area to examine if you want to save some money.

There are many little things you can do to save pennies that add up to dollars. You can lower your electricity bills when it's warmer or put a jacket or sweater on when it's cooler. A lot of this is just becoming more conscious of what things cost and sort of having your own "meter" running. So your gas and electric bills can be watched more closely and you may see that you're saving $20, $30, $40 a month—or more. That's going to help you.

Some people should consider downsizing their house. Or their car. Everybody's at a different place in their life. So there's nothing wrong with buying a new house or a new car if you can handle that. But what you're trying to accomplish is long-term financial freedom

If you really love pulling out plastic, use a debit card tied to your checking account. Best of both worlds.

Two words: skip Starbucks.

Getting out of debt is not only possible, it is vital. You can do this! But you need to approach it like you would a marathon, and not a short sprint. In other words, pace yourself and be patient. I know it's a daunting challenge, but living in denial will just serve to make matters worse.

You need to learn to defer gratification and be willing to make short-term sacrifices in the pursuit of long-term success. You have the power to dig yourself out of debt—use it!

Spending habits die hard, especially when they are ingrained in us from culture and even our family backgrounds. We often need to be relieved of financial anxiety. But nothing changes if nothing changes. We need to start focusing on specific behavior changes, the kinds that take real commitment to implement. Over time, they can become routine because of daily practice.

I firmly believe that giving and getting out of debt go hand in hand. When we put the Kingdom of God first, well, things have a way of falling place. Jesus said it this way:

> *"But seek first his kingdom and his righteousness, and all these things will be given to you as well."*
>
> —MATTHEW 6:33 (NIV)

Habits like tithing, paying cash for purchases, simplifying our lifestyle, and focusing beyond just "right now," can not only turn your finances around—they can turn your whole life around!

Chapter Five

"Your Safety Net"

The COVID-19 pandemic made a lot of bad things worse for many Americans. It was a major game-changer on so many levels. And it remains to be seen how many long-term changes in how people live will come from it.

Of course, it should come as no surprise that many have taken a financial hit. And as the kind of inflation we haven't seen in at least four decades starts creeping and then roaring back, our money is becoming worth less and less. Prices for everyday things like food have soared.

Never has there been a better time to get your financial house in order and to set some compelling goals for the future. And that means one word that can really change your life—savings.

Modern Americans know little about saving money. That's the tough truth. And the recent pandemic has made it worse. It may come as a surprise to you (or maybe not) that 40% of all Americans have less than $300 in savings, and that amount is lower than in recent years.

Experts further tell us that 50% of Americans have less than $600 in savings, and 60% of Americans have less than $1,000 put away.

This means that even small and unexpected expenses that come along, things like repairing a car or a small medical bill, can rock a family's world. And when it comes to younger Americans, paying all their bills in full at the end of a month is a challenge. So people depend more and more on credit cards and that debt spiral I talked about earlier puts them in a hole from which it is difficult to escape.

In chapter two I talked about giving and savings, and I touted the idea of paying yourself ten percent of everything you earn. In other words–socking it away. Your willingness to save money can be a litmus test as to your larger financial health.

And to make matters even worse, most Americans had to dip into those meager savings during the pandemic, which is, of course, understandable. I've talked to so many people about this and they all say they wish they had saved more money before the crisis. But we should always save because there is always a crisis coming.

I firmly believe that everyone needs to have their own safety net and not rely on the government or other entities for help when bad times come. What this means in practical terms is this: You should have three-six months of your annual income in some kind of savings account and one-three months of your income as a balance in your checking account.

This may sound like a daunting task if you are living from paycheck to paycheck right now, but it is very doable. And it will change your life.

You can clean your own house. You can wash your own car. You can do fitness at home. You can find free fun, like parks and picnics, bonfires, and hiking. You can have a garage sale to make extra money. You get all that junk out of there. Get rid of the fancy coffee shops, look for cheaper gas, buy unbranded products and clothes. Most wealthy people don't, they really care about branded stuff. You watch Most of them wear t-shirts and sneakers.

Revisit your insurance premiums, take a brown bag to work, revisit your internet bill, change phone subscriptions. If you have to carpool, that's good. I mean, the list just goes on and on and on, but those are things to save money on are out there. Your cable bill can probably be cut in half. Even if you have to stop the cable for a week and come back as a new subscriber.

There are so many ways to save a little here and there, and it all adds it up to big dollars.

Wall Street

Let's talk a little bit about the stock market. This subject scares some people, but it shouldn't.

Well, we live in the information age, anything that you need to know, you can find on the internet, even using your smartphone.

The first thing you need to know upfront is this: anytime someone's trying to sell you something, take their information with a grain of salt. Because they're there to help themselves, not necessarily you.

If you're going to be in the market (almost everyone is) you should take a page from Warren Buffett's book and "buy and hold." Financial markets are not linear, they're cyclical. They go up and down. Don't panic. If something goes down temporarily it will come back up. But if you sell, it's never going to come back up. Remember this, you never really lose money on an investment that has declined until you actually sell it.

Markets do bounce around with these big fluctuations, which we saw a lot during the COVID. And it can unsettling. I know that. I also know they're based on monetary policy and the Fed (Federal Reserve Board policies, etc.).

Of course, things have changed over the years. These days our American markets, as well as the overall economy, is much more attached to the world market. So a big company in China that goes bankrupt can really put a lot of markets in a tailspin. But you got to hold on as an investor. You can't panic. If you panic and sell, you've lost your money. You need to have a long-term, long-range mindset. Work on developing that.

Study the market. Read the Wall Street Journal every day, as well as following podcasts and blogs on the internet. You can learn a lot in a short period. Sure, you could trust the experts, but wouldn't it be better to become a savvy investor, the kind who can ask financial advisors the right questions?

As investors, you got to understand what's going on with the companies and funds you invest in. And do your best to buy into something when it's at the lower end of the cycle. There is no wiser financial advice than this: Buy low—sell high. And if you just remember that principle, you're going to be all right. Because then you aren't going to panic. I mean, it's pretty simple.

By the way, it's a good rule of thumb that the older you get, the more conservative you should be about investments. You can be more aggressive, even risky when you're young. But that might not be the smart thing as you get older. And be aware of the fact that the older people get the more they become targets of con artists and scammers. It's really sad when you think about it. But you see it in the news all the time about how some 90-year-old widow lost her life savings to some charlatan.

The bottom line is this: You need a safety net of about 3-6 months of your income in savings, and another 1-2 months of your income in your regular checking account. Make this a priority. If you do this, you'll begin to see light at the end of your financial tunnel.

And it won't be a train coming the other way.

Chapter Six

"Straight Talk"

Let's talk about millionaires. There are approximately 17 million millionaires in the United States. They aren't at all what you see on television or in the movies. They don't run around flaunting their money. They aren't braggadocios. Most of them millionaires are average Joes, and they are around you every day. You just don't notice them.

Of course, some flashy cats try to look the part. They're the ones who walk into the room with the big *Starbucks* cup as if it is part of their hand. They carry fake purses, thinking it tells people they're rich. They aren't. They've bought a knockoff. But that isn't wealth—not even close.

But you can easily become rich and it might surprise you how.

Consider a $50 bill. It bears the image of Ulysses S. Grant. Do you realize that if you saved $50 every month and were to earn 15% interest for 40 years, it would grow to a million dollars? If you're 20 years old, it's something you might want to seriously consider.

Most of us assume that millionaires are not like the rest of us—they live differently. And, of course, some do. But there is a difference between the mega-rich like Bill Gates or Jeff Bezos and what I would call the "everyday average" millionaire who may indeed live next door to you. And it may surprise you how these people live their everyday lives.

The average millionaire spends $35,000 on a car. Why do most of us spend more—but we shouldn't. The average millionaire paid less than $400,000 for the home they live in. Even though they could afford much more, they have stayed in the same house. In fact, the average millionaire has lived in the same home for more than two decades—even with an average net worth of $1.8 million at the age of 58.

Check *this* out. Of all millionaires, 20 percent live in a house worth between $400,000 and $600,000. What happens is millionaires upgrade their properties?. They sell their property and take the tax-free money to scale up.

First-time home buyers go out and buy a house for $400,000 to $600,000 and they're tapped out because they've maxed out their budget. However, their neighbor—the unassuming millionaire—has six and a half times more wealth, and he's just cruising because he doesn't have any monthly payments. Do you see what's going on there?

Of course, television and movies show something different. If you watch sports stars and celebrities like that, they're wearing $2,000 and $3,000 suits. But for the average millionaire, the suit costs $500. His shoes cost $200. And his watch costs $300. Most millionaires aren't running around flashing *Rolexes*.

In corporate America, people think if they get a *BMW* or *Mercedes* or get a fancy high-end watch, they are on a roll. But when those payments start rolling in, they're in trouble. And if they're married, it can get even worse. The average millionaire spends $50 on a pair of jeans and $150 on a pair of glasses.

Of Fords & Toyotas

When I first started teaching this in the late 90s, the most common vehicle for a millionaire was a *Ford F-150* pickup. They were the most common. Most millionaires, 9.4 percent, owned a *Ford. Toyotas* represented 5.1 percent, and *BMW's* made up 2.2 percent.

Fast forward twenty years later and the most common vehicle for a millionaire, 12.5 percent, was a *Toyota*, 11.4 percent drove a *Honda*, 9 percent owned a *Ford,* 6.4 percent a *BMW,* and only 3.8 percent sported a *Mercedes.* Most millionaires aren't driving expensive and flashy cars. They want dependable cars to take them from *A* to *B*, because, to them, cars aren't assets.

I drive a 20-year old car. I have a truck that is 16 years old. I have another truck that is 19 or 20 years old. I really don't care about it. Millionaires don't care what you think.

Most people spend their retirement and anything their children would otherwise inherit. But the Bible says, Proverbs 13:22: *"A good person leaves an **inheritance** for their children's children, but a sinner's wealth is stored up for the righteous."*

If you don't like the fruit in your life right now, you're going to have to change things, because if nothing changes, nothing changes.

God wants you to be blessed. He wants you to be able to bless your kids. If your babies need shoes, He doesn't want you struggling. Go get your baby some shoes. But if you don't control your spending, it'll never happen. If you don't manage your money, it will never happen. Money isn't the problem—it's money management. God made us all managers.

A Power Principle—Plant in Your Own Ground

Have you ever heard of a power-principle? This is a power-principle, and this is where so many Christians get messed up. Have you ever been up in Northern California or back east where you see field after field? You see corn and wheat. All that ground is fertile, but you have to plant in your own ground. If you don't plant in your own ground, that isn't on God—it's on you. You can't go on someone else's property and get their crops.

How do you know where your ground is? Well, your ground is your local church, and your ground is when Holy Spirit comes upon you and says, "You need to do this." A lot of churches and ministries have fertile ground, but if it's not your field you will not receive the harvest. Only when you get that inner witness is that your fertile ground. When you give your FIRST ten percent to your local church, that is also your fertile ground. I would go as far as saying that the first ten percent you give to your local church is HOLY GROUND.

When you plant like this, you find synergy with the Father. When you start giving to God's kingdom, all of a sudden the best deals and opportunities start coming your way. Stuff begins to fall into your lap.

Some time ago, I was at a meeting in a local city hall, and a guy walked in. He said, "Excuse me. I'd like to give my house to the city." I said, "Oh, time out, stop right here. Sir, I'll be right back with you." I said, "Can I talk to you real quick?"

We went outside. It turns out that his wife's grandmother died and left them a house. They didn't know what to do with it, so they were going to give it back to the city. It was in bad repair.

Now, I'm a building contractor. It's what I do. This is my lane. I said, "Hey, I'll tell you what I'm going to do. Let's go look at it. I'm going to pull the profile on it to see what's going on with the property."

I said, "This is what I'm going to do. Tonight, I'm going to show up, I'm going to give you a $1,000 down payment, and

I'm going to give you $10,000 grand total for the house. Once we get the transfer into your name, then I'll buy it and transfer it in my name."

I ended up buying a duplex for $10,000 plus fees. Not only did I do that, but I learned how to go through the probate system. So not only did I buy that property, but I learned about a whole new avenue for income—how to get people through the probate system when they inherit property.

I put about $15,000 into it. Three years later, I sold it for $120,000. That's a 400% profit on my investment. Not too bad.

Why did that happen to me? Was it just random and a matter of chance or luck? No way. It was God's blessing because I'm first and foremost an investor in his Kingdom.

What's Your "Talent"?

Are you familiar with the Parable of the Talents? We find it in the Book of Matthew 25:14-29:

> *"Again, it will be like a man going on a journey, who called his servants and entrusted his wealth to them. To one he gave five bags of gold, to another two bags, and to another one bag, each according to his ability. Then he went on his journey. The man who had received five bags of gold went at once and put his money to work and gained five bags more. So also,*

the one with two bags of gold gained two more. But the man who had received one bag went off, dug a hole in the ground and hid his master's money.

"After a long time, the master of those servants returned and settled accounts with them. The man who had received five bags of gold brought the other five. 'Master,' he said, 'you entrusted me with five bags of gold. See, I have gained five more.'

"His master replied, 'Well done, good and faithful servant! You have been faithful with a few things; I will put you in charge of many things. Come and share your master's happiness!'

"The man with two bags of gold also came. 'Master,' he said, 'you entrusted me with two bags of gold; see, I have gained two more.'

"His master replied, 'Well done, good and faithful servant! You have been faithful with a few things; I will put you in charge of many things. Come and share your master's happiness!'

"Then the man who had received one bag of gold came. 'Master,' he said, 'I knew that you are a hard man, harvesting where you have not sown and gathering where you have not scattered seed. So I was afraid and went out and hid your gold in the ground. See, here is what belongs to you.'

"His master replied, 'You wicked, lazy servant! So you knew that I harvest where I have not sown and

gather where I have not scattered seed? Well then, you should have put my money on deposit with the bankers, so that when I returned I would have received it back with interest.

"'So take the bag of gold from him and give it to the one who has ten bags. For whoever has will be given more, and they will have an abundance. Whoever does not have, even what they have will be taken from them.

One guy gets five talents. Another guy gets two talents. The last guy gets one talent. The king leaves. He comes back. The guy with five talents doubles his talents. He says, "Well done, good and faithful servant." The guy with two talents doubles it. He says, "Well done, good and faithful servant."

But the guy with one talent said, "You're a hard master, and I know you reap where you don't sow, and you take things where you didn't give, so I put your money in the ground, and here's your money." He said, "You're a wicked and evil servant. You should have at least put it in the bank." Put your $50 a month in the bank. He said, "Take the money from that one-talent and give it to the 10-talent."

What Jesus said goes against what so many people think.

God expects us to double our money, or end up losing it. That's Bible. I didn't write it. I'm just the messenger. We need to invest in ourselves. We need to be life-long learners. We have to learn about money. We have to be readers. If you don't like where you are, you can fix it. We have to put ourselves in a place where we can act on an opportunity.

Minimum wage was never designed to be a living wage. The minimum wage was designed for teenagers and college students and retired people who got bored at home who had to make under their Social Security limit so they wouldn't get taxed. Social Security was not designed to be your retirement income. It was designed to be supplemental. Hopefully, when it comes time for you to retire, you will have more than your Social Security, because $1,200 a month isn't very much—certainly not enough to live on.

Someone is always watching you. There's someone around you who can meet your need and bless you. They're watching your actions. They're watching how you respond. They're watching your needs. If you dishonor them, though, they're gone. Watch who you dishonor, because once you dishonor people, they seldom come back. They won't necessarily tell you—they just move on. There are also people watching you, who are thinking about leaving you an inheritance, but if you squander every dollar you have, you're a poor investment. Think about it, someone is probably not going to leave you hard-earned money so you can just squander it in a self-indulgent way. That's not a very good return on investment.

Remember, God uses people to bless us.

If you have a hard time keeping a job, you have to look in the mirror and have an honest conversation with yourself. If you're contentious, judgmental, hard to get along with, and always trying to push your opinion or agenda when it's not wanted or accepted, the job isn't the problem—you are.

Get real with yourself and fix that behavior. Be the kind of person other people want to be around. You don't always have to be in control and have it your way. Lighten up, you will ruin more relationships over selfish and controlling emotions than anything else. Learn to work with people.

I was online one day, and I saw a story about someone I knew who was in need. He and his single mom were struggling. Of course, I remembered how my waitress mom raised five kids. So I invited him over to my house so I could tutor him one-on-one about finances.

After about five minutes, it was clear to me that he wasn't really into what I was saying. Fifteen minutes later, he was completely shut down. He didn't want to hear what I had to say because he wanted me to hold his hand and take care of things for him. But I was telling him where it all starts. Wealth is built like a block wall. You do the foundation, you put the steel in, and then it's block by block, block by block, block by block.

Very few people get rich quickly. Sure, there are superstars, movie stars, and *Lotto* winners. But have you ever noticed that a lot of those guys wind up broke? That's because they have no clue how to handle and manage their money. They buy big houses and stuff that have big tax bills. But did you know that for every million dollars you spend on a house, you at least have $1,000 a month in property taxes, not counting other expenses? So when the money stops flowing, those tax bills keep coming.

Keep account of those types of expenses. If you don't get the basics down, you will probably never become financially free. Smart people learn from their mistakes—but wise people learn from other people's mistakes

They Don't Live Like That

You show me someone with high consumption and I'll show you someone with no or little investments.

High consumption involves someone who's into *everything*. They're going everywhere. Money is just flying out of their pockets like in a cartoon. Genuinely wealthy people— average millionaires—don't live like that. They never *have.* Wealthy people are frugal. They look at prices, not because they have to but because it's their mental habit. They're frugal like that. They buy simple stuff. A lot of them don't wear name-brand clothes.

Have you ever noticed that the people in the $2,000 and $3,000 suits work for the people wearing tee shirts? You see Warren Buffett and a lot of those types—there isn't a *Google* brand on them. No *Gucci.* They aren't wearing any of that. They're just average Joes. Warren Buffett eats at *McDonald's* every day. If the stock market is up, he eats a $3.19 meal. If it's down, he eats a $2.59 meal. His company could buy *McDonald's* 50 times over. He just makes a choice every day to be frugal.

You aren't what you drive. You aren't where you live. You have to spend less than you make. Otherwise, it will never work. God has given seed to each sower according to their own ability. If you go back down to the Book of Matthew, it'll tell you that. He gave money to them *according to their ability.* Until your ability grows, you will never achieve financial freedom. Never.

It gets worse. If *you* don't do it, how are your children going to? Your grandchildren? It starts at home. People are following us. We're building a kingdom. People in the church are following us. If we run around broke, disgusted, down on life, we aren't going anywhere. And In the end, we all put our pieces back in the box, and someone else takes it over. Did you leave your mark? Did you fortify your children and your grandchildren?

That's brutal—but it's the truth.

Chapter Seven

"More Straight Talk"

Markets go up and down. Whether it is stocks, precious metals, commodities, or real estate—there are cycles. And learning how to discern and exploit those cycles is crucial when it comes to wise investing.

When is the best time to make money? To have money to use when other people don't.

Consider the story of Joseph P. Kennedy, the father of President John F. Kennedy. Whatever you may think of him—or them—the old man was a savvy investor and a real wizard when it came to growing and managing wealth.

The elder Kennedy was born back in 1888 in Boston to an Irish immigrant family. His father was a politician in the city and that's how Joe learned first-hand about things like making deals, getting inside information—all the skills that make for effective politics. But Joe didn't follow in his father's political footsteps.

He went into business.

Starting out on Wall Street, he became the president of a bank when he was only 25 years old. But it was the stock market where he made his fortune. He used what he learned from his father about how to use "inside" information. Of course, nowadays that would be illegal, but back then, the market was a wide-open field like the old wild west.

During the 1920s—the decade that roared—he got rich. Then he got richer because he had the sense to get out of the market just before the big bubble burst—the big crash of 1929 that ushered in the Great Depression. He had been smack dab in the middle of all the mania during the market's decade-long rise, but getting out just in time left him with a large pool of cash which he used to scoop up bargains for pennies on the dollar.

There is a story about Joe and the 1920s stock market. Days before the crash, a certain moment lead him to liquidate his portfolio. Why? One day while he was getting his shoes shined, the shoeshine boy gave him some stock tips. Kennedy wisely surmised that when the shoeshine boys have hot tips, the market is probably too good to be true.

Kennedy had acquired his fortune when stocks soared. But, more importantly, he managed to preserve that fortune and build on it when almost everyone else was losing everything. He bought real estate and made other investments when prices were at historic lows. And his net worth went from a pre-crash $30 million to an amount that would be equal to several *billion* dollars in today's values.

And the rest, as they say, is history.

Oh, and Joe Kennedy had a saying that is worth considering when it comes to making and selling investments: "Never hold out for top dollar."

Keep an Eye on Washington

One thing to watch closely when it comes to discerning the best investments to make and the best timing for them is what the government is doing. This is because when Washington touches something it tends to get messed up. Usually when they claim to be "helping the poor," it's more about lining their own pockets.

Remember during the pandemic how the government was giving money away left and right? They extended unemployment and increased payments. What happened? Now, so many people don't want to go to work and there are millions of job openings left unfilled.

While that was all going this could be a good time to buy a house or houses. Because, in the wake, of the rental crisis, and with all the government payments, property values soared and rental prices have increased. If you had hit it just right, you could have made a bundle. That's, of course, if you had some cash to work with. But you didn't need much, because interest rates for mortgages remained low.

The aftermath of this stimulus package has not come into full effect yet, but when it does there will be some great opportunities. You will not need a lot of money to get into a property either. Maybe about 3% or 10% down will get you into a house. There will also be some great opportunities to start or buy a businesses

These are the kinds of things to watch for. If you have the cash to work with, then when things go "on-sale" if you are in a position to pick up some bargains. And when you put God first, He has a way of bringing the power of synergy into your life.

The Big Tenth

Look at the idea of tithing. You give away ten percent as an act of faith. God is moved by faith. He's not moved by our emotions. But He loves obedient faith. In effect, He says: "Do you believe me enough to give your first ten percent to support the church? I just need someone to believe me. If you believe me, I will bless you. I'll throw stuff your way—so much that you can't even imagine it."

Why does He want to do that? Because He needs the church to be *whole*. We need families to be whole to keep the church whole because we're building a kingdom.

One day I was sitting in a church staff meeting (I was there on assignment for a year). Someone said that a guy had finished his first year of Bible College, but he couldn't afford the next year. They wanted to know if the church, or someone else, could pick it up the second year for him. But no one stepped up to pick up the tab.

Right then, the Holy Ghost hit me—Boom! I said, "I'll pay it." What no one knew at that time I was getting paid two times a month from the church. The first check paid all of my bills, but the second one I stuck in my pocket. I was double—even triple-dipping, as far as streams income were concerned. At that time, I was also working in law enforcement, and still running my construction company

Remember that Power Principle, the one about planting in your own ground? When I left that meeting, I paid that Bible College bill. I did so because the Holy Spirit prompted me to. It was *holy ground*. That ground was fertile for planting.

In less than two hours a real estate agent called me. She said, "Dale, I have this lot in Grand Terrace, three-quarters of an acre. Would you like to look at it?" An hour later, he accepted my offer of $10,000 plus fees. It was a lot worth $100,000. I live on the property today.

That's synergy—but you don't get that without becoming a giver. I don't say these things to brag but to encourage you, if God will do something for others He will do it for you.

Paying Yourself?

Shifting gears a bit, let me mention something else. Everyone seems to be paying the rent man, the phone man, the car man, the utility bill, the Starbucks bill—but are they paying *themselves*. Are you? If you get to the end of the month and you haven't paid yourself, you've messed up. You're the most important person in the equation. Pay yourself.

How much should be paying yourself? Well, the rich reinvest 15 to 20 percent of their income, across the board. You should start with ten percent. Of course, if you are in debt up to your eyeballs, you will find it hard to pay yourself. You can't live at the rate of 120 percent of your income and make any real progress toward acquiring wealth. So start where you are.

When you are rich, you work for *assets*. Poor people work for money. What is God's money? Way back when, it was things like land, cattle, gold, silver, livestock, and crops. By the way, these are still good investments in our day and age. But where do most people put their money? Starbucks, new cars, and such, and they're tapped out.

We need a paradigm shift. Instead of trying to act and look rich, let's start living like the rich. And in a few short years, you *will* be rich. I could write another whole book on the blessings of the LORD and what HE has done for me down through the years. And one day you will be able to do the same—if you serve HIM and follow HIS ways.

Invest—Where?

Where should you be invested? Let's start with putting $50 in a mutual fund. You can find one through *Fidelity, Vanguard,* and *T. Rowe Price.* Maybe in a growth fund, or a growth and income fund. Most of them are up to 18 to 20 percent in the last ten years. Maybe you work for a company that matches funds. You should certainly max that out. Even the military will do this.

Let's say you make $19 an hour—or about $36,500 per year. Five percent is $165 per month. If your employer matches it, that leverages your investment. So, that's $330 per month or nearly $4,000 annually. Doing that for 30 years will more than make you a millionaire. Why aren't you already taking advantage of that?

Well, maybe it's because you are going to Disneyland a lot, eating chocolate-covered bananas and sipping lattes at Starbucks. You get what I mean. Spend, spend, spend without saving for the future.

You could also buy a house or pay off the one you have now

I once turned a $32,000 investment into almost a quarter of a million dollars in just five years. I bought a piece of property. When? At the bottom of the cycle. I sold it for $182,000. Here were the terms: $47K down, the seller carries a note for the rest back at 5.5% for 15 years. I get a payment of $1,103 per month—that's $13,236 over a year.

Why would I do it that way?

One word—*taxes*. I receive about $13K per year for 15 years and that adds up to $189K. The principle is $135K, so the interest is about $63K. By taking this in payments spread out over time I saved about $20K on capital gains taxes also.

That's what I mean by working for *assets*.

You see, people who work for money pay 20, 25, or 30 percent in taxes. But capital gains are only 15%. This is the reason people like Warren Buffett pay such a low rate of tax. Some politicians or talking heads on television made say that the rich don't pay taxes, but they do. They just pay them according to a different calculation.

Watch this. If I put $750 per month into an investment for 15 years, at 15% from those monthly payments I get, it can grow to $508,000. That means it will double again into a half million. So it would turn 32,500 to 500,000 in 20 years. At that point, I would use the rest of the payment to pay my tithe and taxes

The bottom line is that this is all very doable.

For anyone.

Chapter Eight

"Become a Life-Long Learner"

The late great automaker Henry Ford said, "Anyone who stops learning is old, whether at twenty or eighty. Anyone who keeps learning stays young. The greatest thing in life is to keep your mind young."

Mr. Ford was on to something. Something very important. I believe it is vitally important to your ultimate success to be a life-long learner. Too many people think they need to learn stops when your "formal" education is finished. But that's simply not true—at least it shouldn't be.

It used to be widely believed that our development peaked at about the age of 25, but there is more and more evidence that supports the value of learning even well into our old age. This is because as the years advance, we don't just acquire new knowledge, we can blend it with practical experience from life-long observation. What this leads to is that wonderful word: Wisdom.

Consider what scripture says in the Book of Proverbs:

"Blessed are those who find wisdom, those who gain understanding."

—PROVERBS 3:13

"Get wisdom, get understanding; do not forget my words or turn away from them."

—PROVERBS 4:5

"The beginning of wisdom is this: Get wisdom. Though it cost all you all have, get understanding."

—PROVERB 4:7

"For through wisdom your days will be many, and years will be added to your life."

—PROVERBS 9:11

"How much better to get wisdom than gold, to get insight rather than silver."

—PROVERBS 16:16

"By wisdom a house is built, and through understanding it is established."

—PROVERBS 24:3

The fact is that more and more people who thought they had left learning in their rear-view mirrors are finding out that school can be lovelier the second time around. Maybe some are thinking of new streams of income, but for the most part, this is about keeping their minds alive and well.

Protect Your Brain

Part of the motivation seems to be based on science. You see, the fact is that exercising the brain may very well save it. It is a powerful tool to put off mental decline, possibly even Alzheimer's disease or dementia.

The late Steve Jobs once gave a speech at Stanford University where he talked about this idea of life-long learning. He called it "connecting the dots." By that he meant that all of our life experiences can be learning experiences and what we learn can be useful somewhere else in our lives. And if you think about your own life, you can likely find examples of this.

So when you are experiencing something, ask yourself: "What can I learn from this?"

How does more formalized education play into this idea of being a life-long learner? Well, if it's related to your craft, you need to be everything you can do. You need to get as many degrees as you can get because once you get a master's degree and a doctorate in a real field, you will usually have a job. You'll have insurance and a retirement plan and that's another source of income.

However, it's important to remember that formal education may be a good place to start, but it's a bad place to stop. That's because most highly-educated people are working for business owners who don't have near as much formal training. But they are, in fact, always learning.

Maybe you have a mental block when it comes to "classroom" education, sitting and listening to a lecture. I get that. It's like Winston Churchill said, "I have always enjoyed learning, but I have never enjoyed being taught." You're going to find that the best educational experiences are well outside the "formal" classroom.

Frankly, there is always something we can learn. It could be a new hobby or even a new career. When you consciously commit to becoming a life-long learner, you will embrace new challenges to discover new things. And there are many great benefits when you do this.

Knowledge is Power

First, as I've already mentioned, you can help your brain stay strong and healthy by looking for new things to challenge you.

Being a consumer of information can also help you with your current job. When you learn new things, you are, in effect, acquiring new skills. And often, those skills can translate to promotions and new career opportunities.

Barbara Oakley is a professor of engineering at Oakland University in Rochester, Michigan and she wrote a book titled, *Mindshift: Break Through Obstacles to Learning and Discover Your Hidden Potential.* She told a story about someone who worked at a university in Holland. This person helped her career through her passion for online video gaming. Although she didn't really think of this as any kind of second skill, certainly not a marketable one, she wound up using it to become the manager of her school's online curriculum. She created systems and strategies based on her gaming experience.

Stories like that prove that we never really know where our "expertise" will come in handy.

Life-long learners tend to be happier people. This is because it tends to improve our emotional life with a sense of personal fulfillment. And, as we get older, we tend to be more prone to depression. Most of us know elderly people who battle this. But keeping our minds sharp through a consuming hunger for knowledge is a sure way to push back on that kind of depression.

In fact, learning might even help you to live longer.

Getting Started

So, how do we become life-long learners? One word: Read. Leaders are readers and readers can be leaders, it's as simple as that. It's been said that you will be the same person in five years as you are today, except for the books you read and the people you meet.

You're reading a book right now. Why? Because you want to learn. But do you realize how important regular reading is? There are mental and even physical benefits to turning pages on a consistent basis. They range from better concentration to even sleeping better. Consider these:

1. Reading can help you with decision-making. Getting older certainly impacts our decisiveness. We become increasingly dependent on others. Older people need help with decisions, but this doesn't mean that they want to be indecisive. No. They love independence. Well, exercising the brain with reading can help.

2. Reading can help with things like Loneliness, Depression, and Anxiety. Because reading helps us to relax, it acts as a distraction from the things that stress us out.

3. Reading can help us with Sleep issues. As we get older, it's easier to suffer from sleep problems such as insomnia. But the simple act of picking up a book can make falling asleep much easier. This may sound simple and basic, but it's very true. And it's amazing how many people miss this.

4. Reading can help us with Memory issues. While memory loss is a common thing as we age, reading a book, and the concentration it requires, can actually improve our memories.

5. Reading tends to improve our moods. Have you ever noticed how some people seem to get grumpy as they get older, while others are jolly? The difference is often as simple as reading books.

What are some other ways to incorporate life-long learning into your life?

You could *learn a new skill.*

You could *learn a new language.*

You could start *listening to podcasts.*

You could start *keeping a journal.*

You could *sign up for a course* at a local college.

You could *join a club*—maybe even a book club.

Don't Forget to Look Here

Albert Einstein (certainly a life-long learner) said this: "Wisdom is not a product of schooling, but of the life-long attempt to acquire it." The man with the crazy hair nailed it.

Edward Paxton Hood was a preacher in England in the nineteeth century, and he said this: *"Our whole life is an Education—we are ever learning, every moment of time, everywhere, under all circumstances something is being added to the stock of our previous attainments. Mind is always at work when once its operations commence. All men are learners, whatever their occupation, in the palace, in the cottage, in the park, and in the field. These are the laws stamped upon Humanity."*

Indeed.

By the way, the greatest source of knowledge is a book called the Bible. I probably should have put this first, but it's true. Don't ever make the mistake of thinking the Bible is about "religious stuff." Did you know that Jesus talked more about money matters than he did about heaven and hell combined?

As you look to your future, make sure it incorporates a commitment to life-long learning. Knowledge is power, and once you get it anything is possible. You can even learn from the negative things that will happen.

Emerson said, "The mind, once stretched by a new idea, never returns to its original dimensions."

It's time to start stretching your mind—today!

Chapter Nine

"Multiple Streams of Income"

Have you ever thought about starting a side-gig? This may surprise you, but nearly fifty percent of all Americans count on funds from a source of income other than their primary jobs to make ends meet. And get ahead. In fact, developing multiple streams of income is becoming a major way people prepare for those golden retirement years, as well as paying off large debts—things like a home mortgage.

Finding new streams of income can help you have a "safety net" in place in case bad things come your way. Things such as losing your job or, God forbid, becoming seriously ill. This safety net can be there when you find yourself temporarily unable to fully support yourself and your loved ones.

Financial security should be your goal. And when your "9 to 5" job pays the regular bills, you can use income from other streams to make investments and build a bigger nest egg. Who wouldn't like to have an extra $10K or $20K in reserve?

One of the other great things about finding and tapping into auxiliary sources of income is that you can pay down your debt, and even retire large debt early, usually saving a lot of interest. Most of us would love to have our house paid off long before we reach retirement age.

Wouldn't you like to be able to have funds socked away for things like that new transmission, or the deck you want to build behind your house, or even the approaching Christmas season? Wouldn't it be great not to have to depend on high-interest credit cards when facing those "special" expenses? Multiple streams of income can be a big help.

By the way, a side-gig doesn't always have to be just about the money. Many of us long for an outlet for our creative side. And turning that hobby into a money-maker can be quite enjoyable.

Multiple streams of income can help us get the earning vs spending equation into balance. And this means more money for your future goals and dreams. And it means you'll have more to take a few risks down the road.

Of Streams & Side-Gigs

A side-gig could be a part-time job for a company or business, or it could be more "entrepreneurial"—meaning something you do self-employed. Of course, multiple streams of income can also involve investment income, interest from savings, dividends from stocks, or even rent or royalties from other properties you own. The most common sources of non-job related income are:

- Funds from some outside source, for example, royalties on a book you've written.
- Funds generated by something you own that other people want to use. Things like rental property.
- Funds that flow from traditional investments, like your stock portfolio.
- Funds generated by running your own side business.

The idea is to have other sources of income and not to be totally reliant on your primary job or paycheck. Of course, all potential side-gigs, or alternative streams of income involve a measure of risk. But there is a saying, "Go out on a limb, that's always where the fruit is."

While it's true that, for the most part, you have to spend money to make money, you don't have to front large amounts of money to begin earning returns. But investments can be difficult at times. Their value to you as an additional stream of income depends a lot on your particular situation. Factors such as how much income you desire, as well as the timeline you need to accumulate it are vital.

I believe, when it comes to investment, you need to think long-term. There is an old Japanese proverb, "Money grows on the trees of patience."

The legendary investor and financial expert Warren Buffett is famous for his standing advice to "buy and hold" stocks and other investments. He is a fountain of wisdom when it comes to making good investment decisions.

Buffet—the "Oracle of Omaha"—says that we don't feel comfortable owning a stock for at least a decade, we shouldn't bother owning it for ten minutes. Here are a few other gems of wisdom from Buffett:

"Rule number one: Never lose money. Rule number two: Never Forget rule number one." Of course, Buffett has lost money himself, as he did famously during the big financial meltdown back in 2008, when his losses topped $23 billion (yes, billion with a "b"). But what he means by his "rules" is that we should look at investments as gamblers would. We should study the companies in which we invest and do our due diligent homework. Buffett invests in companies only after he has studied them enough to completely understand them.

Another Buffett gem is: "If the business does well, the stock eventually follows." He has made a career out of looking for businesses that have solid business plans and consistent operating histories. In fact, he never buys a single share unless he can take a pen and paper and list the reasons he is willing to pay a specific price for shares of a specific company.

Here's another: "It's far better to buy a wonderful company at a fair price than a fair company at a wonderful price." Quality and value are flip sides of the same point to Mr. Buffett. He looks for businesses that provide a solid and reliable service or product. For him, finding the right business at the right price is the ballgame.

Solid advice from the man who is likely the world's greatest investor in stocks.

What About Property?

When it comes to acquiring and managing income-producing property, you can make good money particularly in markets with a strong rental history. It can be as simple as renting out an extra bedroom, or even having something available on Airbnb. Maybe you can acquire a vacation home and rent it out when you don't plan to use it. Or you could even invest in an apartment building.

But real estate can be quite expensive—to acquire and even maintain. So you should proceed with caution. Oftentimes, this particular stream of income becomes viable after a couple of other streams have given you some "capital" to leverage.

Starting your own side-business is a common income producer. It can also be the most fulfilling. And it is easier these days than it has ever been. You see, time was that when you wanted to start a business you needed to rent a space and stock some shelves with products. But now, you can get a business up and running with no more than getting a domain name on the internet and maybe a few registration fees.

In fact, most people who "freelance" run a small business even without taking steps to formalize things (incorporation, etc.). People write blogs, create podcasts, start *YouTube* channels, and other things that can be used to generate income. They usually start with a subject they're passionate about. This helps because running a business requires a large measure of commitment and dedication. So enjoying the work becomes important.

And passion always sets you apart in any sphere or marketplace.

Practical Ideas

Finally, here are a few ideas—areas where you might be able to pick up some extra cash and tap into the power of multiple streams of income:

- Some single moms have become pet sitters or even baby sitters.
- You could become a virtual assistant to help someone else run a business or market a product.
- You could start a blog and find ways to monetize it.
- Maybe you could be a freelance writer—or proofreader, or copywriter.

- How about buying and "flipping" large ticket items, like cars or furniture.

- How about online tutoring?

- You could be a transcriptionist (they're in demand).

- Become a ride-share driver (*Uber*, *Lift*, etc.)

- Are you handy? You could market your "handyman" services

Frankly, the list can be as long as there are ideas that people are passionate about. People who save money earn interest. Songwriters get royalties. Authors do, too. Insurance and security agents get residual business. Even actors get their cut of the project. Franchisors get fees. Software creators, game designers, and other inventors and creative types get royalties. You get the drift.

The point is, having more than one way to make money is often the key element of eventually finding financial freedom and security.

Chapter Ten

"Preparing for Your Golden Years"

If you are like most people, you aren't really thinking much these days about how life will be for you in your so-called "Golden Years." I'm talking about retirement. The simple fact is, the earlier you focus on this the better those years yet to come can be for you.

In fact, some people don't think about retirement until they are just about ready to stop working—or find themselves in a position where they are forced to retire.

One thing to consider, whatever your retirement plans, is that most of us will live longer than our great-grandparents lived. And those "Golden Years" could actually become golden *decades.*

Good Old Social Security

Consider that one part of most retirement plans—Social Security. Do you realize that when that program was started back in the 1930s the life expectancy for men was 58 years, and for women, it was 62. And the retirement age was 65. Do the math. It's pretty clear from those early stats that Social Security was never meant to be a complete retirement plan. I mean, it makes for a nice supplement later in life, but you will never really collect enough to live on. You should know that when you're younger.

Frankly, most young people I talk to—people in their 20s and 30s—tend to believe that Social Security, as we now know it, will not be there for them in 30 or 40 years. And they may be right. The numbers simply don't lie. It's not a program that can sustain itself, at least not without major restructuring.

Due Diligence

So, what exactly should we be doing to plan for later? Well, I think the first thing is developing a measure of literacy when it comes to financial matters. Do you have the ability to deal with economic information in order to make good, informed decisions? This is all part of that "life-long learning" value I've written about.

Frankly, it just makes sense that you need a basic grasp of financial issues and how various "products" work to effectively prepare for retirement. This is vital because we can't really leave such planning to experts or agents. They can be helpful, but it's always better to do our due diligence—meaning homework.

There are several things to consider as you start planning. First, when do you plan to retire—at what age? The answer to this question is important because your age when you stop working will greatly affect how much money you will need.

Second, you will need to prepare for your tax situation in retirement. Yes, retirees still pay taxes. In fact, in many cases, Social Security benefits are taxed. Does that surprise you? Well, it's true.

What About Healthcare?

Another consideration is your healthcare situation down that road. Of course, the whole issue of healthcare is big and controversial these days, and who knows what those "great minds" in Washington will continue to do to foul everything up. But the bottom line is that healthcare will be a huge deal when you retire.

Well, you may think Medicare will take care of everything. Now, it is an essential and valuable program that helps millions of Americans. However, it can be complicated. Do you know about part A, or B, or even D? And did you know that how much you make in retirement can impact what you pay monthly, even for Medicare? By the way, yes—people pay for Medicare. It's cheaper than traditional health insurance, but if you want a good health plan after leaving your job with its benefits, you need to do your homework.

A Smooth Transition

Another thing to prepare for is exactly how to make a smooth and seamless from work to retirement. You might want to consider is maybe phasing into retirement by starting with a "part-time" retirement from your job. You may be surprised how open some employers are to this. After all, you will have knowledge and experience, and you be well-equipped to train others who are coming up the ladder behind you.

Sometimes employers can see this as a way to reduce the disruption caused by sudden changes in staffing. This is why many retirement-age employees transition to full retirement via a few years of "consulting" type of work. This kind of "knowledge transfer" can be a great benefit to a company.

Whatever process you envision for retirement—be it instant or phased in—reaching that pinnacle of your working life should be a time worth celebrating. However, often it brings with it worry because most people don't really have enough money to make it work.

So exactly how do you avoid a train wreck when you arrive at those "Golden Years?" Well, there's an old saying: "Failing to plan is planning to fail," and it is never more true than when it's applied to preparing for retirement.

The earlier you put "plan-for-retirement" on your to-do list, the better.

When Do I Start?

Here's the best retirement advice you'll ever receive: START NOW! But whenever you start, you need a strategy. The first thing you need to learn about is something called a 401K. That moniker is based on language in the IRS tax code. Basically, this allows you to take some of your regular paycheck and designate it for retirement, and you don't pay any income taxes on that set-aside money until you start to draw it at retirement. It's a sweet deal, and as I mentioned earlier in this book, many companies have a matching program where they add money to what you've set aside. Add to this the power inherent in something called "compound interest," and you have a prescription for real retirement success.

That's a sweet deal on steroids.

By the way, the amount you can put in your 401K has increased as of 2022. In some cases, you can put up to $20,500 in such an account.

Of course, another important thing about retirement is to pay off your debt. When you reach the age where you want to stop working every day, having a debt burden makes full retirement almost impossible.

So how much will you need when you retire. Well, there are many good "retirement calculators" out there. Do some homework. For many of them, you simply plug in your age and then your planned age of retirement. Other factors include investment patterns and risk aversion

Take, for example, the case of a 30-year-old man who wants to fully retire at age 65. If you save (via 401K, etc.) $10,800 per year, you'll have about $48,200 per year to live on in retirement (this includes Social Security). So you can see the benefit of starting early.

You might need some help with that but choose your financial advisors carefully. There are solid brokerage firms like *Vanguard Fidelity, Charles Schwab, T. Rowe Price*, and *E-Trade*, and they have great mutual funds. So if you just put a couple of hundred bucks in one of these tried and true growth and growth and income funds, you'll probably do pretty well.

Here's the takeaway: Find a good retirement calculator and start filling in the blanks. Don't delay. Your future is at stake.

Just imagine living life without a house payment or a car payment, or credit card payments. Imagine how free you would be. You would have no pressure and the ability to seek and fulfill the plan of God for your life without financial "issues." You can do this. The choice is yours.

How Do You Want to Spend Your Retirement Time?

I have a brother who retired a while back from law enforcement. But he didn't just decide to go fishing or sit in a recliner to wither away. He works in a food ministry at his church, feeding those in his community who are in need. He donates his time—two or three days a week. (and loves every minute of it) But he can do this because he has a steady stream of retirement income.

I have another brother who retired from the same department in Southern California, and he is handling things differently. He spends his time working with wood, making things like benches. He loves that kind of work. He also has a steady stream of retirement income.

Now, we could debate the relative merits of serving in a food ministry versus building stuff, but the fact is that both men have the freedom to do what they want. Why? How? They prepared for it.

I should add that working in law enforcement and construction has been our family business. In fact, I worked in that field for a number of years. I happened to work as a correctional officer in a state prison. But I found a way to pursue another passion along the way also. I have had a little construction business for about 30 years now. I also have been an ordained minister for more than two decades, and I have built many churches on the mission field.

It actually grew quite a lot. I was eventually working on a large, $18 million church project, and I had to decide to let one of the jobs go. So it was good-bye prison guard. I love being a business owner.

My brothers, however, chose to stay on the law enforcement path for 30 years. Freedom to choose is a beautiful thing. And financial freedom makes it even better.

Do you ever think about what you want to do when you stop working in whatever career you're in? Let's say that you have put all your ducks in a row, and you will have a nice, livable stream of income coming your way when you retire.

Some people spend a lot of time thinking about *where* they will retire, but when it comes to retirement, where is not really as important as *what*. As in, *what will you do?*

The transition to retirement is not all that easy for many people. Sure, retirement sounds great in theory, but when you actually face it, things can be a little unsettling. There are, in fact, several types of retirees.

Some retirees find ways to continue doing what they did on the job, but in a different, or at least modified way. For me, I've been a builder, and maybe I'll dabble in that some when I am done with full-time work.

Other retirees are determined to get as far away from their old work habits as possible. They've decided that retirement is time to try new things, a time for adventure. They look for new hobbies. They travel a lot. Maybe they take a class at a local college on a subject they know nothing about.

Yet other retirees just want to enjoy themselves, but not in a sedentary way. They don't schedule much and live in the moment from day to day. They've worked hard, maybe even built a great business, but now they want no pressure. But they don't want to vegetate or rusticate. They want to be active, but not in a highly-structured way.

I think the key is this: ACTIVITY. Keep moving and never stop.

Remember this as you plan for those "Golden Years," retirement should be all about FREEDOM and CHOICE. We all want the choice part, but the fact is that to be able to truly choose how we want to spend our later years, we must be financially secure.

Don't waste another minute. Get ready for later—NOW!

About the Author

Dale Chronister is a general contractor, church builder, and equipper of the saints. He loves to mentor the people around him in the areas of business and finance. His hobbies include off-roading and cruising. But his greatest passion is learning and teaching about the things of God and his Son Jesus Christ. Dale lives in a little Southern California city called Grand Terrace.

A Note from Dale

Throughout this book, I've talked about my faith. I want you to know that you can have a real relationship with God. The Bible tells us that whosoever calls on the name of the LORD shall be saved (See: Romans 10:13). If you have never done this, I urge you to call on His name today! Ask JESUS to forgive your failures, shortcomings, and sins, and invite Him to come into your heart and be the Lord of your life.

— Dale

Made in the USA
Columbia, SC
14 February 2022